christmas sweets

christmas sweets

hamlyn

NOTES

Standard American cup measurements are used in all recipes.

1 cup = 8 fl oz	½ cup = 4 fl oz
⅓ cup = 3 fl oz	¼ cup = 2 fl oz

Medium eggs have been used throughout.

A few recipes include nuts or nut derivatives. It is advisable for those with known allergic reactions to nuts and nut derivatives and those who may be potentially vulnerable to these allergies, such as pregnant and nursing mothers, invalids, the elderly, babies and children, to avoid dishes made with nuts and nut oils. It is also prudent to check the labels of prepared ingredients for the possible inclusion of nut derivatives.

Ovens should be preheated to the specified temperature. If using a convection oven, follow the manufacturer's instructions for adjusting the time and temperature.

First published in Great Britain in 2004 by Hamlyn,
a division of Octopus Publishing Group Ltd
2–4 Heron Quays, London E14 4JP

ISBN 0 600 61284 8

A CIP catalogue record for this book is available from the British Library

Printed and bound in China

10 9 8 7 6 5 4 3 2 1

contents

Introduction

Christmas is a time for friends and family, for celebrating in relaxed surroundings with those close to you. This enjoyable time of year is marked by rituals and traditions wherever you are in the world, and this usually includes feasting.

This is the time of year when many people like to treat themselves and their loved ones with home-baked sweets, such as cookies, cakes, and candies. People who rarely bake at other times of the year are often tempted to do so at Christmas to keep the traditions alive. Christmas baking is very satisfying, and homemade cakes and pastries are universally popular, whether eaten at home or given as a delicious gift.

Christmas ingredients
Wherever they originate, traditional Christmas sweets are often made using the same ingredients.
• **Nuts**, such as Brazils, pecans, and almonds, are used in cakes, pastries, and cookies.
• **Cranberries** are often served in a savory sauce along with the Christmas turkey, but they can also make a wonderful ingredient in sweet recipes such as muffins.
• **Dried fruits**, such as raisins, dried candied peel, and dates, are used to make many festive foods, such as Christmas cake, traditional Christmas pudding, and mince pies.
• **Marzipan** (almond paste) is used for decoration or to make a sumptuous stuffing for cakes.
• **Spices** are very popular and transform Christmas sweet treats with their exotic flavors. Cinnamon, nutmeg, ginger, and cloves add aroma and spice to many different dishes.

Traditional foods

Most countries that celebrate Christmas have their own Christmas cake. In the United States and Britain, it is a rich fruit cake, sometimes covered with marzipan and decorated with icing. In France, it is a *Bûche de Noël*, a chocolate log cake symbolizing the yule log, which was once kept burning throughout the 12 days of Christmas. The Italians make Panettone, a light sweet bread enriched with dried fruits, while the Germans enjoy Stollen, a yeast cake with dried fruit, sometimes stuffed with marzipan.

Nowadays, many people have a more modern take on Christmas foods. What about offering your visitors a Reindeer Cupcake or a Snow-covered Ginger Muffin? This book contains plenty of wonderful recipes for seasonal fare, from the truly traditional to those with a contemporary twist.

Family fun

Christmas preparations offer a great opportunity to get the whole family involved, regardless of age. The anticipation and preparation are often as enjoyable as the main event, and it's a good way to channel all that pre-Christmas excitement and get the kids to work off steam. Most families have their own traditions and it is these rituals, such as baking the same muffins every year, or decorating the Christmas tree, that make the fondest memories.

One reliable source of family fun is to make your own edible Christmas decorations. They look beautiful, they taste good, and they are fun to make. Even very small children can help cut out the cookie shapes or hang them up with ribbon. It also offers an opportunity for creative expression—even if you do end up with clashing colors and gaudy finishing touches. This is the one time of year that a bit of bad taste is acceptable and all part of the fun.

Baking cookies for Santa is another lovely activity for keeping traditions and beliefs alive. Again, it is one where children can take an active role, and gives the adults something to nibble when the kids are in bed. Children can help make the cookies, then put them on a plate and leave them out for Santa to enjoy when he delivers the gifts on the stroke of midnight. Don't forget to leave him a drink—milk, hot cocoa, cider, mulled wine, or something stronger...

Edible gifts

Everyone loves homemade cookies and sweets, and they are always gratefully received as gifts at Christmas-time. People really appreciate the effort involved in making them, and they are usually far superior to their store-bought counterparts. Consider mouth-watering cookies such as Ginger Snowmen, Mulled Wine Cookies, and Sweet Biscotti. Or what about scrumptious sweets such as Chocolate Cherry Fudge, Marrons Glacés, Sugar Plums, or Champagne Truffles?

Choosing attractive packaging for edible gifts is very important, and enjoyable too. Look out for pretty gift boxes and line them with tissue in matching colors to keep the cookies or sweets from moving around and getting damaged. Alternatively, buy a roll of scrunchy cellophane and use to wrap the sweet treats, securing with invisible tape and festive ribbons and bows. If necessary, add a pretty tag with detailed storage instructions and a "best before" date.

Christmas drinks

As well as all the traditional Christmas foods, there are seasonal drinks too. For the ultimate in comfort, curl up by the fire with a winter warmer such as Egg Nog or Festive Hot Chocolate. This book also contains recipes for a range of tempting cold drinks, such as Cranberry Crush, which will be enjoyed by family and friends alike and is great for serving at parties.

Christmas traditions

Traditions and rituals vary around the Christian world as people celebrate Christmas in their different ways. The United States and Great Britain share many customs including carol singing and Christmas stockings. Another shared tradition is that of the Christmas tree, a custom that originated in Germany. Advent calendars also came from Germany. They used to consist of 24 little boxes hanging on a fir wreath, each containing a tiny gift, but nowadays they are more likely to be made of cardboard with little windows to open, counting down the days to Christmas Day.

The main focus of the festive period is Christmas dinner, usually served at lunchtime on Christmas day. This is generally roast turkey, followed by pecan or mince pies and plum pudding. Traditionally the pudding was made a month before Christmas and every member of the family took a turn in stirring the mixture, while making a wish. Small silver coins or charms were hidden in the pudding, bringing luck to those who found one in their portion.

In France, the main celebration is held late on Christmas Eve, or in the early hours of Christmas morning after mass. These days, turkey and chestnuts are popular, but many still prefer a goose. In the southeast, the meal always finished with the 13 Christmas desserts, symbolizing the 13 present at the Last Supper. These are *pompe à l'huile* (fruit pastry), raisins, quince paste, marzipan sweets, nougat, *fougasse* (rich cake), crystallized lemons, walnuts and hazelnuts, pears, plums, dried figs, almonds, and dates.

Italians fast on Christmas Eve until after Midnight Mass, when they have a grand feast, which often includes *cotechino*, a fresh pork sausage served with lentils. Traditional Dutch Christmas foods are carp, small spicy cakes called *spéculos*, apples, which represent the tree of knowledge, and nuts, symbolizing life's hardships, while Scandinavian festive foods include fruit-filled pastries and cakes, braised ham, and marinated fish.

1⅓ cups **unbleached all-purpose flour**

¼ cup **superfine sugar**

1 teaspoon **ground ginger**

7 tablespoons **butter**, cut into pieces

24 small **edible silver balls** or **tiny sweets**

4 oz ready-to-use **white rolled fondant*** or **marzipan (almond paste)**

pink and blue food coloring

small tube **black writing icing**

Frosting:

1 cup **confectioner's sugar**

1 pinch **ground ginger**

5 teaspoons **water**

Makes 12
*Preparation time: **30 minutes***
*Cooking time: **7–8 minutes***

Ginger snowmen

These crisp shortbread cookies flavored with just a hint of ginger are sure to delight any young child.

1 Preheat the oven to 350°F. Put the flour, sugar, and ginger into a mixing bowl or a food processor. Add the butter and rub in with the fingertips or blend until the mixture resembles fine crumbs.

2 Continue mixing, or form the ingredients into a soft ball with your hands. Knead lightly, then roll out thinly between two pieces of parchment or wax paper.

3 Cut out snowmen shapes using a 4-inch cookie cutter and transfer to ungreased baking sheets. Bake the snowmen for 7–8 minutes until pale golden. Leave to cool on the baking sheets then transfer to a wire rack set over the sheets.

4 To make the frosting, sift the confectioner's sugar and ginger into a bowl. Gradually mix in the water until you have a smooth frosting. Spoon over the cookies and allow to drizzle over the edges. Position the silver balls for eyes, then leave to dry and harden.

5 To complete the decoration, color half of the rolled fondant icing pink, the other half blue. Roll out on a surface dusted with a little confectioner's sugar and cut out strips for scarves. Drape the scarves around the snowmen's necks. Reroll the trimmings and cut semi-circles for the hats and shape small balls for the pom poms. Add to the snowmen, sticking the pom poms with a little water. Pipe on small, black, smiling mouths. Leave for 1 hour to harden before serving.

*Ready-to-use rolled fondant is available through cake decoration supply stores and online specialty retailers.

¼ cup **crunchy peanut butter**

7 tablespoons **butter**, at room temperature

⅓ cup **raw sugar**

1⅓ cups **self-rising flour**

1–2 tablespoons **milk**

Makes 16
Preparation time: **20 minutes**
Cooking time: **8–10 minutes**

Peanut butter cookies

These soft, buttery cookies taste deliciously warm from the oven. If you plan to leave some out for Santa, hide them from the rest of the family.

1 Preheat the oven to 350°F. Lightly butter 2 baking sheets. Put the peanut butter, butter, and sugar into a mixing bowl or a food processor and beat until smooth.

2 Mix in the flour and add enough milk to make a smooth dough. Use your hands to shape teaspoons of the mixture into balls and arrange them, spaced apart, on the prepared baking sheets.

3 Bake the cookies for 8–10 minutes until cracked and golden. Allow them to harden for a minute or two, then transfer to a wire rack to cool. These cookies are best eaten on the day they are made but can be stored in an airtight container for up to 4 days.

Mulled wine cookies

With the warm, spicy flavors of mulled wine, these cookies make a great accompaniment to coffee—perfect for serving to friends and neighbors who drop in during the holidays.

1 Put the raisins and cranberries into a small heavy saucepan with the wine, jelly, and spices. Heat until the jelly dissolves, then bring to a boil and boil for 2–3 minutes until the syrup is reduced by about half. Allow to cool.

2 Preheat the oven to 350°F. Lightly grease a large baking sheet. Mix the nuts and chocolate in a bowl with the flour, orange zest, melted butter, egg, and fruit mixture to make a paste. Place teaspoons of the mixture, spaced slightly apart, on the prepared baking sheet.

3 Bake the cookies for about 20 minutes until they have spread slightly. Leave them on the baking sheet for 3 minutes, then transfer to a wire rack to cool. Dust generously with confectioner's sugar. They can be stored in an airtight container for up to a week.

½ cup **raisins**

⅓ cup **dried cranberries**

½ cup **red wine**

½ cup **redcurrant jelly**

1 pinch **chili powder**

1 teaspoon **ground cinnamon**

¼ teaspoon **ground cloves**

¼ cup **walnuts**, chopped

¼ cup **whole, blanched almonds**, chopped

3½ oz **plain dark chocolate**

⅔ cup **self-rising flour**

finely grated zest of 1 **orange**

¼ cup (½ stick) **unsalted butter**, melted

1 **egg**

confectioner's sugar, for dusting

Makes 25
*Preparation time: **15 minutes***
*Cooking time: **25–30 minutes***

6 tablespoons **butter**

¼ cup **golden syrup**

scant ½ cup **superfine sugar**

1 teaspoon **ground cinnamon**

½ teaspoon **ground ginger**

1 large pinch **ground allspice**

2⅔ cups **unbleached all-purpose flour**

1 teaspoon **baking soda**

3 tablespoons **milk**

4-oz tube **white decorating icing**

few **edible colored cake decorating balls**, optional

Makes 25
Preparation time: **40 minutes**
Cooking time: **15–17 minutes**

Tree decorations

The wonderful aroma of cinnamon, ginger, and allspice that pervades the house while these festive cookies are baking sums up the spirit of Christmas-time. This is a great activity for children to join in.

1 Preheat the oven to 350°F. Lightly grease 3 baking sheets. Put the butter, syrup, and sugar into a saucepan and heat gently, stirring occasionally, until the butter has melted and the sugar dissolved.

2 Take the pan off the heat and stir in the spices. Mix together the flour and baking soda then beat into the spicy butter mixture, adding enough milk to make a smooth dough.

3 Turn out the dough on to a board and leave for 5–10 minutes until cool enough to handle. Knead well then roll out on a floured surface or a piece of parchment or wax paper.

4 Cut out festive shapes using star-, stocking-, reindeer-, Santa-, and bell-shaped cookie cutters. Transfer the shapes to the prepared baking sheets.

5 Make a hole in the top of each cookie with the end of a toothpick or a teaspoon handle and bake for 10–12 minutes until browned. Enlarge the hole for ribbon if needed. Allow to cool on the baking sheets.

6 Pipe the frosting on to the cookies, add the colored balls, if using, and let harden. Thread fine ribbons through the holes on the cookies and tie on to the Christmas tree. Eat within 2 days.

TIP
If the children take a long time cutting out the cookies, you may need to soften the dough in the microwave for around 20 seconds before rerolling.

⅔ cup (1 stick plus
2 tablespoons) **butter**

1 cup **superfine sugar**

few drops of **vanilla extract**

1 **egg yolk**

1 tablespoon **milk**

1 generous pinch **ground
cardamom**

1 generous pinch **ground
cinnamon**

finely grated zest of ½ **lemon**

½ cup **ground almonds**

1½ cups **unbleached
all-purpose flour**, sifted

4 oz **plain dark chocolate**,
chopped

Makes 15
Preparation time: **20 minutes**,
plus chilling
Cooking time: **15 minutes**

Sweet biscotti

**These chocolate-dipped Italian cookies make a pretty and sophisticated
gift at Christmas. Pack in colored cellophane bags and tie with ribbon.**

1 Beat the butter in a mixing bowl
with the sugar and vanilla extract
until pale and creamy. Add the egg
yolk, milk, spices, lemon zest, and
almonds and knead the sifted flour
into this mixture. Chill in the
refrigerator for 1 hour.

2 Form the dough into rectangular
logs, about 1½ inches in diameter,
wrap in foil, and chill in the
refrigerator for 2 hours.

3 Preheat the oven to 375°F and
grease a baking sheet. Cut the
blocks of dough into ¼-inch slices,
place on the baking sheet and
bake for 15 minutes. Remove the
cookies with a metal spatula and
cool on a wire rack.

4 Place the chocolate in a
heatproof bowl and melt over a
pan of gently simmering water. Dip
the cookies into the chocolate so
that they are half coated and allow
to cool on parchment or wax paper.
The biscotti can be stored in an
airtight container for up to a week.

Chocolate hazelnut cookies

Speckled with chunky pieces of hazelnut and diced chocolate, these dark chocolate cookies are best served while they are still warm from the oven—a real festive treat.

1 Preheat the oven to 350°F and grease 2 large baking sheets. Put the cocoa powder in a small dish and mix to a smooth paste with the boiling water.

2 Cream the butter and sugars in a bowl until light and fluffy. Add the cocoa paste and a little of the egg and beat well. Mix together the flour and baking soda then mix in alternately with the remaining egg.

3 Stir in the chopped chocolate and nuts. Drop teaspoons of the mixture, well spaced apart, on to the baking sheets. Bake the cookies for 8–10 minutes until golden. Allow to harden for a minute or two then transfer to a wire rack to cool. These cookies are best eaten soon after making but they can be stored in an airtight container for up to 4 days.

4 teaspoons **cocoa powder**

5 teaspoons **boiling water**

7 tablespoons **butter**, at room temperature

⅓ cup **raw sugar**

⅓ cup **superfine sugar**

1 **egg**, beaten

1⅓ cups **unbleached all-purpose flour**

½ teaspoon **baking soda**

3½ oz **plain dark chocolate**, finely diced

⅓ cup **blanched hazelnuts**, chopped

Makes 24
*Preparation time: **30 minutes***
*Cooking time: **8–10 minutes***

7 tablespoons **butter**

½ cup **maple syrup**

¼ cup **superfine sugar**

1 teaspoon **baking soda**

1 **egg yolk**

1⅓ cups **unbleached all-purpose flour**

¼ teaspoon **ground cinnamon**

3 oz **plain dark chocolate**, broken into pieces

3 oz **white chocolate**, broken into pieces

Makes 40
*Preparation time: **20 minutes**,*
plus setting
*Cooking time: **12–15 minutes***

Maple cookies

Dipped in chocolate, these delectable maple cookies are thin and crisp. Serve with mugs of coffee or hot chocolate for a mid-morning treat.

1 Preheat the oven to 375°F. Melt the butter in a saucepan, then let it cool slightly.

2 Stir the maple syrup, superfine sugar, baking soda, and egg yolk into the melted butter then mix in the flour and cinnamon. Beat until you have a smooth creamy dough.

3 Drop teaspoons of the mixture, spaced slightly apart, on a baking sheet lined with parchment paper. Bake the cookies for 4–5 minutes until golden brown. Let them harden for a minute or two then transfer to a wire rack using a metal spatula and leave to cool. Continue until all the mixture has been used.

4 Place the plain chocolate in one heatproof bowl and the white chocolate in another. Set them over a pan of gently simmering water and allow to melt.

5 Hold one of the cookies over the bowl and spoon a little of the chocolate over half of it, spreading it with the back of the spoon. Return the cookie to the wire rack and coat all the cookies in the same way. Leave in a cool place for 30 minutes until the chocolate has hardened then pack into an airtight container, separating the layers with sheets of parchment paper. The cookies can be stored for up to 2 days.

TIPS
For a change, use honey instead of the maple syrup, or ground ginger in place of the cinnamon. Try sprinkling broken brown sugar clumps over the cookies just before cooking, instead of coating them in chocolate.

⅞ cup (1¾ sticks) **unsalted butter**, at room temperature

scant ½ cup **superfine sugar**

1¾ cups **unbleached all-purpose flour**

½ teaspoon **baking powder**

scant ¼ cup **cocoa powder**

2 teaspoons **milk**

3½ oz **plain dark chocolate**, broken into pieces

Makes 12
Preparation time: **15 minutes**
Cooking time: **15–20 minutes**

Chocolate Viennese whirls

A chocolate version of buttery little Viennese whirls, these little cookies are set in pretty cake cases and filled with melted chocolate after baking.

1 Preheat the oven to 375°F. Line a 12-cup muffin pan with paper baking cups. Beat together the butter and sugar until pale and creamy. Sift the flour, baking powder, and cocoa powder into the bowl, add the milk and beat well to make a smooth paste.

2 Spoon the mixture into a piping bag fitted with a large star nozzle and pipe swirls into the paper cases, leaving a large cavity in the center.

3 Bake the whirls for 15–20 minutes or until slightly risen. Press a hole in the center of each one. Allow to cool in the pan.

4 To decorate, place the chocolate in a heatproof bowl and melt over a saucepan of gently simmering water. Spoon a little chocolate into the center of each whirl. Allow to set slightly before serving.

Chocolate macaroons

Crisp on the outside and moist inside, little chocolate macaroons make a stylish accompaniment to coffee after Christmas dinner.

1 Preheat the oven to 350°F. Line a large baking sheet with parchment paper. Whisk the egg whites until stiff, then gradually whisk in the sugar until the mixture is thick and glossy. Gently fold in the ground almonds and grated chocolate.

2 Put the mixture in a large piping bag fitted with a large plain nozzle and pipe small rounds, about 1½ inches in diameter, on to the baking sheet. Alternatively, place small teaspoons of dough on the baking sheet.

3 Press a chocolate-covered coffee bean into the center of each macaroon. Bake for about 15 minutes until slightly risen and just firm. Leave the macaroons on the paper to cool. Store in an airtight container.

TIP
Chocolate-covered coffee beans are available from some supermarkets and specialty coffee shops. If you can't find them, decorate each cookie with a whole blanched almond.

2 **egg whites**

scant ½ cup **superfine sugar**

½ cup plus 2 tablespoons **ground almonds**

2 oz **plain dark chocolate**, grated

25 **chocolate-covered coffee beans**, to decorate

Makes 25
*Preparation time: **10 minutes***
*Cooking time: **15 minutes***

7 tablespoons **butter**, at room temperature

¼ cup **golden syrup**

⅓ cup **raw sugar**

⅔ cup **unbleached all-purpose flour**

½ teaspoon **baking soda**

1 teaspoon **ground ginger**

⅓ cup **rolled oats**, plus extra for sprinkling

Makes 20
*Preparation time: **20 minutes***
*Cooking time: **8–10 minutes***

Oatmeal cookies

This is a comforting, old-fashioned cookie that keeps well and is ideal to have on hand for unexpected guests.

1 Preheat the oven to 350°F. Lightly grease 2 baking sheets. Put the butter, syrup, and sugar into a bowl and beat until light and creamy.

2 Mix the flour with the baking soda and ginger, then gradually beat it into the creamed mixture. Stir in the oats.

3 Drop heaping teaspoonfuls of the cookie mixture, spaced well apart, on the greased baking sheets. Sprinkle with a few extra oats and cook for 8–10 minutes until golden.

4 Let the cookies harden for a minute or two, then transfer to a wire rack to cool. They can be stored in an airtight container for up to 4 days.

Linzer cookies

These rich hazelnut shortbreads have a just a hint of lemon and a ruby-red jam filling. Tiny heart- and star-shaped cutters can be used to cut out the centers of the cookies.

1 Preheat the oven to 325°F. Grind the hazelnuts very finely in a blender or coffee grinder.

2 Put the flour and sugar into a mixing bowl or a food processor, add the butter and rub in with your fingertips or process until the mixture forms fine crumbs.

3 Stir in the ground hazelnuts and lemon zest, then mix in the egg yolk and bring the mixture together with your hands to a firm dough.

4 Knead lightly on a work surface dusted with a little flour. Roll out half the dough to $^1/_2$-inch thickness and cut out $2^1/_4$-inch rounds with a fluted cookie cutter. Arrange on an ungreased baking sheet. Use a cookie cutter to remove 1-inch hearts and stars from the centers of half of the cookies.

5 Bake the first batch of cookies for about 8 minutes, until pale golden brown. Meanwhile, roll out the second half of the dough and cut shapes as before. Reroll the trimmings, cutting out shapes until all the dough has been used, and bake as before. Leave the cookies on the baking sheets for a minute or two to harden, then transfer to a wire rack to cool.

6 Divide the jam between the centers of the whole cookies and spread thickly, leaving a border of cookie showing. Cover with the hole-cut biscuits, dust with a little sifted confectioner's sugar and let them cool completely before serving. The cookies can be stored in an airtight container for 2 days.

¼ cup **hazelnuts**

2 cups **unbleached all-purpose flour**

$^1/_3$ cup **superfine sugar**

$^2/_3$ cup (1 stick plus 2 tablespoons) **butter**, cut into pieces

finely grated zest of ½ **lemon**

1 **egg yolk**

¼ cup **seedless raspberry jam**

confectioner's sugar, to decorate

Makes 16
Preparation time: **35 minutes**
Cooking time: **16 minutes**

2 cups **bread flour**

1 teaspoon **active dried yeast**

2 teaspoons **superfine sugar**

large pinch of **salt**

1 tablespoon melted **butter** or **sunflower oil**

scant ½ cup warm **water**

3 oz each **plain dark**, **white**, and **milk chocolate**, broken into pieces

Glaze:

2 tablespoons **water**

½ teaspoon **salt**

Makes 40
*Preparation time: **30 minutes**, plus rising and setting*
*Cooking time: **6–8 minutes***

Triple chocolate pretzels

These dainty bread morsels are brushed with their traditional salt glaze before baking, and then drizzled with dark, white and milk chocolate to make eye-catching petits fours.

1 Preheat the oven to 400°F. Lightly grease 2 large baking sheets.

2 Mix the flour, yeast, sugar, and salt in a bowl. Add the melted butter or oil and gradually mix in the warm water until you have a smooth dough. Knead the dough for 5 minutes on a lightly floured surface until it is smooth and elastic.

3 Cut the dough into quarters, then cut each quarter into 10 smaller pieces. Shape each piece into a thin rope about 8 inches long. Bend the rope so that it forms a wide arc, then bring one of the ends around in a loop and secure about half way along the rope. Do the same with the other end, looping it across the first secured end.

4 Transfer the pretzels to the greased baking sheets. Cover loosely with lightly oiled plastic wrap and leave in a warm place for 30 minutes until well risen.

5 Remove the covering. To make the glaze, mix the water and salt in a small bowl until the salt has dissolved then brush this over the pretzels. Bake for 6–8 minutes until golden brown. Transfer to a large wire rack and leave to cool.

6 Place the dark, white, and milk chocolates in 3 separate heatproof bowls and melt over pans of gently simmering water. Using a spoon, drizzle random lines of dark chocolate over the pretzels. Leave to harden then repeat with the white and then the milk chocolate. When set, transfer to an airtight container and eat within 2 days.

2¼ cups **granulated sugar**

1½ cups **water**

2 tablespoons **golden syrup**

2 tablespoons **butter**

½ cup **heavy whipping cream**

2 oz **plain dark chocolate**, broken into pieces

scant ½ cup **red candied cherries**, roughly chopped

Makes 30 squares
Preparation time: **10 minutes**
Cooking time: **15–17 minutes**

Chocolate cherry fudge

This rich dark chocolate fudge, speckled with vibrant red candied cherries, looks festive and tastes delicious too. It makes a great stocking filler, or an ideal gift for school friends.

1 Put the sugar, water, and syrup into a heavy saucepan and heat gently, without stirring, until the sugar has dissolved. Meanwhile, lightly grease a 7-inch shallow cake pan with a little of the butter.

2 Add a sugar thermometer to the pan and increase the heat. Cook until the thermometer reads 225°F. Stir in half of the cream and heat for 2–3 minutes until the temperature reaches 238°F.

3 Mix in the remaining cream and heat for about 5 minutes until the temperature reaches 240–245°F or a little of the syrup forms a soft ball when dropped into a bowl of cold water. Keep a watchful eye over the fudge as it cooks, and stir more frequently as the heat increases so that the fudge does not stick and burn.

4 Take the pan off the heat, let it cool for 2–3 minutes then add the chocolate and the remaining butter. Stir constantly for 3–4 minutes until the chocolate and butter have melted and the fudge begins to thicken and look grainy. Stir in the cherries then pour the mixture into the prepared cake pan. Let the fudge cool for 10 minutes then mark it into squares and leave to cool completely.

5 Loosen the edges of the fudge from the sides of the pan, turn it out on to a chopping board and cut into small squares. Wrap in squares of colored cellophane and tie with ribbon or raffia. The fudge can be stored for up to 1 week.

Creamy pistachio toffee

This golden toffee is made with heavy whipping cream and green pistachios. Break it into pieces and pack in pretty jars or colored cellophane to make an attractive gift.

1 Put the sugar and cream into a heavy saucepan and heat gently, stirring occasionally, until the sugar has completely dissolved. Meanwhile, use a little of the butter to grease a 7-inch shallow square cake pan.

2 Stir the remaining butter into the sugar and cream mixture, add a sugar thermometer if you have one, and increase the heat. Cook for about 15 minutes until the temperature reaches 290°F or a little of the toffee forms a hard ball when dropped into a bowl of cold water. Stir the toffee occasionally at first, then more frequently as the mixture begins to color and thicken so that it cooks to an even creamy brown and doesn't burn on the bottom of the saucepan.

3 As you continue to heat, the toffee will froth then thicken with a grainy texture. When the butter begins to separate out of the toffee, it is almost ready. Cook for a few more minutes until it changes to a smooth glossy toffee.

4 Take the pan off the heat, quickly stir in the pistachio nuts, then pour the toffee into the buttered pan. Allow to cool for 5 minutes then mark into strips and let cool completely.

5 When cold, loosen the edges of the toffee from the sides of the pan and turn it out. Break into pieces with a toffee hammer or by hitting a cook's knife with a rolling pin. Wrap pieces of toffee in colored cellophane and tie with thin ribbon or raffia. It can be stored for up to 1 week.

1⅓ cups **granulated sugar**

1 cup **heavy whipping cream**

2 tablespoons **butter**

¼ cup **pistachio nuts**, roughly chopped

Makes 30 pieces
Preparation time: **15 minutes**
Cooking time: **20 minutes**

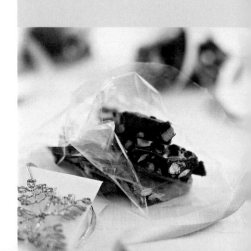

1 cup **mixed whole nuts**, such as **cashews, hazelnuts, pistachios**

10 oz **plain dark chocolate**, broken into pieces

1 tablespoon **butter**

2 tablespoons **confectioner's sugar**

2 tablespoons **heavy whipping cream**

Makes 28
*Preparation time: **40 minutes**, plus chilling and setting*
*Cooking time: **10 minutes***

Rocky road clusters

Pistachios, cashews, and hazelnuts are toasted then coated in dark chocolate to create appealing nut clusters. The jagged shapes look particularly attractive when packed into a mixed box of petits fours.

1 Place the nuts on a baking sheet, then toast in a preheated hot oven for 3–4 minutes until golden. Allow to cool slightly then chop roughly.

2 Meanwhile, place 3 oz of the chocolate in a heatproof bowl and melt over a pan of gently simmering water. Stir the butter, sugar, and cream into the melted chocolate until smooth and glossy, then mix in all but 2 tablespoons of the chopped nuts.

3 Drop rough teaspoons of the mixture on to a baking sheet lined with parchment paper. Chill for 2–3 hours until firm.

4 To finish, melt the remaining chocolate as before. Coat the nut clusters in the melted chocolate by holding them on a fork, one at a time, over the bowl of chocolate and spooning some of it over the top with a teaspoon. When the excess chocolate has dripped away, return the cluster to the paper-lined tray and repeat with the remainder.

5 Put the chocolates in a cool place and leave to set for at least an hour. Sprinkle with the reserved nuts. Transfer them to petit four cases when ready to serve.

TIP
Nuts burn quickly, so don't leave them unattended while toasting.

Champagne truffles

For the ultimate chocolate experience, bite through a brittle chocolate coating to a soft creamy Champagne center.

1 Place half of the dark chocolate in a heatproof bowl and melt over a saucepan of gently simmering water. Stir in the Champagne or sparkling wine, the cream, and the sugar and mix until smooth and glossy. Chill for 4–5 hours or overnight.

2 Using 2 teaspoons, scoop and scrape the soft truffle mixture into rough balls and arrange on a plate. Freeze for 30 minutes to harden.

3 Put the cocoa powder on a saucer and, dipping your fingertips in it regularly, roll the truffles into neat rounds. Return to the plate and freeze again until firm.

4 Melt the remaining dark chocolate as before. Coat the truffles with the melted chocolate by holding them on a fork, one at a time, over the bowl of chocolate and using a teaspoon to spoon the chocolate over the top. When the excess chocolate has dripped away, place the truffles on a baking sheet lined with parchment or wax paper.

5 Chill the truffles for 1 hour until hardened. Melt the white chocolate as before and drizzle or pipe the truffles with white lines. Chill again until the decoration has hardened, then transfer to petit four cases. Arrange the truffles in a small box; they can be stored in the refrigerator for up to 5 days.

10 oz **plain dark chocolate**, broken into pieces

½ cup **Champagne** or **sparkling dry white wine**

3 tablespoons **heavy whipping cream**

2 tablespoons **confectioner's sugar**

2 teaspoons **cocoa powder**

2 oz **white chocolate**, broken into pieces

Makes 20
*Preparation time: **45 minutes**, plus chilling and freezing*
*Cooking time: **10 minutes***

½ cup **heavy whipping cream**

5 oz **white chocolate**, broken into pieces

1 oz (about 2 tablespoons) **strong, hard white peppermints**

⅓ cup **confectioner's sugar**

Makes 20
*Preparation time: **30 minutes**, plus chilling*
*Cooking time: **4–5 minutes***

White chocolate mint truffles

Smooth white chocolate truffles lightly flavored with crushed peppermints are perfect for an after-dinner sweet.

1 Pour the cream into a heavy saucepan and add the chocolate. Heat gently, stirring occasionally, for 4–5 minutes until the chocolate has melted. Allow to cool.

2 Whisk the cream mixture until thick, then chill in the refrigerator for 3–4 hours.

3 Put the peppermints into a plastic bag, crush with a rolling pin then stir into the chilled cream mixture. Drop teaspoons of the soft mixture on to a plate and chill for 1 hour or freeze for 30 minutes until firm.

4 Sprinkle the confectioner's sugar on another plate, then roll the truffles in the sugar to form neat balls. Pack into a small box lined with wax paper and dust with the remaining sugar. Chill for at least 2 hours before serving. The truffles can be stored in the refrigerator for up to 4 days.

VARIATION
Roll the truffles in grated white chocolate instead of the confectioner's sugar. Alternatively, coat them in a solid chocolate shell (see Champagne Truffles on page 29).

10 oz **plain dark chocolate**, broken into pieces

7½ oz **strawberries**

4 oz **red cherries** or **grapes**

2 oz **Brazil nuts**

Serves 4
*Preparation time: **25 minutes**, plus chilling*
*Cooking time: **10 minutes***

Chocolate fruit cups

Little chocolate cases make tempting and impressive containers for dainty sweet fruit and nut treats.

1 Place two-thirds of the chocolate pieces in a heatproof bowl and melt over a saucepan of gently simmering water.

2 Cut out 4 circles of heavy-duty foil, about 8 inches in diameter. Take 1 circle and mold it around an orange or a large apple, fitting it tightly around the base of the fruit and pulling up the edges of the foil to create a cup shape. Carefully remove the fruit and press the foil cup gently on a work surface to make a flat base. Shape the remaining foil circles in the same way.

3 Spoon a little chocolate into one of the foil cups, then spread it around the inside with the back of the spoon. Coat the remaining cups in the same way, using about half the chocolate. Chill for about 10 minutes until beginning to set, then give the cups a second coat with the remaining melted chocolate. Chill for at least 30 minutes until set.

4 Meanwhile, melt the remaining chocolate as before. Half-dip the fruit and nuts in the chocolate and leave to set on a sheet of parchment or wax paper.

5 Use cool hands to peel the foil away from the chocolate cups, starting at the top and working down to the bottom. Fill the cups with the fruit and nuts and keep in a cool place until ready to serve.

Caramelized pecans

Here, pecan nuts are sandwiched with a layer of moist hazelnut marzipan, then coated in a glass-like golden caramel for a professional finish that is easy to obtain at home.

1 Place the hazelnuts on a baking sheet and grill under a preheated grill until lightly browned. Allow to cool slightly, then grind finely in a food processor or blender. Brush a baking sheet with a little oil.

2 Reconstitute the egg white with warm water, according to package instructions, then add the superfine sugar and ground hazelnuts and mix to a stiff paste.

3 Sandwich the pecan nuts together in pairs with a little of the hazelnut marzipan in between.

4 Put the granulated sugar and water in a heavy saucepan and heat gently, without stirring, until the sugar has completely dissolved. Increase the heat and cook for 10–15 minutes until the syrup has turned golden.

5 Plunge the base of the pan into a bowl of cold water to prevent the syrup from cooking and darkening further. Drop the sandwiched pecan nuts, one at a time, into the caramel. Lift out with a fork and place on the oiled baking sheet.

6 Let the pecans cool and harden, then transfer them to petit four cases. They can be stored in an airtight container for up to 4 days. Separate the layers with wax paper.

TIP
If the caramelized nuts are left uncovered, the moisture in the air, especially in a hot steamy kitchen, will soften the coating.

¼ cup blanched **hazelnuts**

oil, for brushing

1 dried **egg white**

¼ cup **superfine sugar**

½ cup **pecan nuts**

1 cup **granulated sugar**

¼ cup plus 1 tablespoon **water**

Makes 35
Preparation time: **40 minutes**
Cooking time: **20 minutes**

1 lb **fresh chestnuts**

1 cup **granulated sugar**

1 cup **liquid glucose**

1 cup **water**

½ teaspoon **vanilla extract**

To finish:

½ cup **granulated sugar**

3 tablespoons **water**

Makes 60

*Preparation time: **40 minutes**,*

*plus standing, **over 10 days***

*Cooking time: **35 minutes***

Marrons glacés

These French favorites are wonderful served with coffee after a meal or used to decorate chocolate desserts and ice creams.

1 Make a small cross-cut in the top of each chestnut shell, then boil for 2 minutes. Peel away the shell and the inner skin with a small knife. If the nuts are hard to peel, return to the pan, bring back to a boil and try again.

2 Put the peeled chestnuts into a pan, cover with cold water, bring to a boil and simmer gently for 20 minutes until just tender. Drain and transfer to a shallow dish.

3 To make a sugar syrup, put the sugar, liquid glucose, and water into a saucepan. Heat gently until the sugar has dissolved, then boil for 1 minute. Pour over the chestnuts, cover with a plate and leave in a warm place overnight.

4 On day 2, drain the syrup into a saucepan and boil for 4 minutes. Pour over the chestnuts, cover,

and leave overnight as before. On day 3, repeat as on day 2, adding the vanilla extract after boiling. On day 4, repeat the sugar boiling process once more. Add the chestnuts, then soak for 3 days.

5 On day 7, arrange the chestnuts in a layer on a wire rack set over a baking sheet. Leave in a warm place for 2–3 days, turning once or twice until the coating is hard.

6 On day 9 or 10, make the glacé finish. Boil some water in a pan. Put the sugar and water in another pan. Heat until the sugar has dissolved, then boil for 1 minute. Using tongs, dip the chestnuts into the boiling water. Shake off the excess moisture then dip into the sugar syrup. Dry the chestnuts overnight on a rack. Wrap in foil and store in an airtight container. They will keep for 3 months.

Sugar plums

These traditional Christmas-time sweets are made with moist chopped dates, golden raisins, dried plums, and cherries and flavored with a little orange zest and brandy. Omit the alcohol if serving the sugar plums to children.

1 Put all the fruits into a food processor or blender and chop finely. Gradually work in the confectioner's sugar, orange zest, and brandy or orange juice until the mixture binds together. If you do not have a food processor, finely chop the fruits and mix in a bowl with the sugar, orange zest, brandy, or juice.

2 Drop spoonfuls of the mixture on to a baking sheet, then roll them between your fingertips to shape into balls. If the mixture seems sticky at this stage, leave it for an hour for the fruits to absorb the brandy or orange juice, then try again.

3 Allow the sugar plums to dry at room temperature for 5–6 hours, then roll them in the superfine sugar and arrange in petit four cases. Store in an airtight container at room temperature and eat within 3 days.

TIP
If you like nuts, substitute 1 cup of the fruit for some chunky, roughly chopped almonds, pistachios, or hazelnuts.

heaping ½ cup **chopped dates**

heaping ½ cup **sultanas** or **raisins**

1 cup **pitted dried plums**

1 cup **candied cherries**, halved

⅔ cup **confectioner's sugar**

finely grated zest of 1 **orange**

2 tablespoons **brandy** or **orange juice**

¼ cup **superfine sugar**

Makes 32
*Preparation time: **20 minutes**, plus drying*

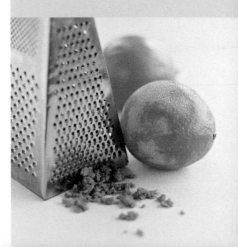

½ bunch **green seedless grapes**

½ bunch **red seedless grapes**

1 cup plus 2 tablespoons **confectioner's sugar**

4–5 teaspoons **orange** or **lime juice**

¼ cup **superfine sugar**

Serves 6–8
*Preparation time: **20 minutes**, plus setting*

Frosted grapes

Complete a special meal and impress friends and family with this dainty dish of frosted fruit. They are quick and easy to make and even young children can help out.

1 Wash the grapes then pat dry with paper towels. Snip into tiny bunches of 2 or 3 grapes.

2 Sift the confectioner's sugar into a bowl, then gradually mix in the fruit juice to make a smooth, thick frosting.

3 Dip the grapes, a bunch at a time, into the frosting then arrange them on a wire rack set over a baking sheet. Leave in a cool place for 1 hour or until hardened.

4 Sprinkle the grapes with the superfine sugar then transfer to petit four cases or arrange on a plate. Eat within 3 days.

TIP
Fresh stemmed cherries and physalis may also be dipped in the frosting.

3½ cups **unbleached all-purpose flour**

1 large pinch of **salt**

1½ teaspoons **active dried yeast**

¼ cup **superfine sugar**

¼ cup **warm water**

3 **eggs** or 6 **egg yolks**

¼ teaspoon **vanilla extract**

2 teaspoons **finely grated lemon zest**

½ cup (1 stick) **butter**, softened

⅓ cup **golden raisins**

3 tablespoons **candied peel**, chopped

melted butter, for brushing

Serves 6–8
*Preparation time: **30 minutes**, plus rising*
*Cooking time: **about 50 minutes***

Panettone

Panettone is a traditional part of Christmas fare in Italy. This sweet, fruited yeast cake keeps well in an airtight container and can be reheated whole.

1 Grease and line a 7-inch round cake pan. Sift three-fourths (about 2½ cups) of the flour and salt into a mixing bowl and leave in a warm place. Dissolve the yeast and 1 teaspoon of the sugar in the warm water and leave to froth.

2 Mix the remaining sugar into the flour. Beat the eggs with the vanilla extract and lemon zest. Stir in the flour, a third at a time, and mix into a soft dough which can be gathered into a ball. Gradually beat in the butter. Add a little more flour, working the dough with your hands into a manageable ball.

3 Turn out the dough on to a floured board and knead for about 10 minutes until smooth and silky, then put it into a warm bowl, cover and leave for 45–50 minutes, or until doubled in size.

4 Punch down the dough and knead in the golden raisins and candied peel. Shape the dough into a ball, put it into the prepared pan and cut a cross in the top. Leave in a warm place for 15–20 minutes or until doubled in size.

5 Preheat the oven to 400°F. Brush the top of the panettone with melted butter and bake for 10 minutes. Brush again with melted butter, reduce the oven temperature to 350°F, and cook for another 40 minutes. The panettone is ready when the top is crisp and golden and a toothpick inserted into the center comes out clean. Cool on a wire rack. Serve cut into thick wedges.

Stollen

Traditionally served at Christmas, this German yeast cake is quite delicious. It is a slow riser because of the large amount of fruit but well worth the time it takes to make.

1 Blend the yeast in the warm water. Dissolve two-thirds of the sugar and the salt in the milk. Add the rum, almond extract, and yeast liquid.

2 Sift the flour into a bowl, making a well in the center. Add the yeast mix, egg, half the softened butter cut into small pieces. Mix to a soft dough and knead for 10 minutes by hand, or 4–5 minutes in an electric stand mixer fitted with a dough hook. Add the fruit and nuts.

3 Return the dough to the bowl, cover with a damp towel and leave to rise in a warm place until doubled in size—about 2 hours.

4 Punch down the dough and knead it until smooth, then roll it out on a lightly floured surface to a rectangle about 12 x 8 inches.

5 Melt the remaining butter and brush liberally over the dough, then sprinkle with the remaining sugar. Shape the marzipan into a sausage the length of the rolled-out dough and add to the center of the dough.

6 Fold one long side over just beyond the center, and then fold over the other long side to overlap the first piece well. Press together lightly and slightly taper the ends.

7 Place the loaf on a greased baking sheet, brush with melted butter and leave in a warm place until almost doubled in size. Preheat the oven to 375°F.

8 Bake the stollen for about 45 minutes. Cool on a wire rack. To serve, dredge heavily with sifted confectioner's sugar and cut into thin slices.

2 tablespoons **fresh yeast** or 1 tablespoon **active dried yeast**

2 tablespoons **warm water**

⅓ cup **superfine sugar**

1 pinch of **salt**

⅓ cup **warm milk**

2 tablespoons **rum**

a few drops of **almond extract**

3¾ cups **unbleached all-purpose flour**

1 **egg**, beaten

⅔ cup (1 stick plus 2 tablespoons) **butter**, softened

¼ cup **raisins**

¼ cup **candied cherries**, rinsed, dried, and chopped

¼ cup **currants**

1 oz **candied angelica**, chopped

¼ cup **candied peel**, chopped

½ cup **flaked almonds**

6 oz **marzipan**

confectioner's sugar, to serve

Serves 6
*Preparation time: **30 minutes**, plus rising*
*Cooking time: **45 minutes***

Tropical Christmas cake

Bursting with color and flavor, this tropical fruit cake makes for an original alternative to traditional Christmas fare.

1¼ cups (2½ sticks) **unsalted butter**

1 cup **superfine sugar**

3 large **eggs**, beaten

3½ cups **self-rising flour**

1 14-oz can **pineapple rings in syrup**

⅓ cup **candied cherries**, chopped

⅓ cup **candied peel**, chopped

3 tablespoons **candied angelica** or **green candied cherries**, chopped

3 tablespoons **walnuts**, chopped

3 tablespoons **dried coconut**

½ cup **golden raisins**

2 tablespoons **toasted coconut shavings**, to decorate

Frosting:

3 tablespoons **unsalted butter**

1½ cups **confectioner's sugar**

2 tablespoons **dried coconut**

Serves 10
*Preparation time: **30 minutes***
*Cooking time: **1¼–1½ hours***

1 Preheat the oven to 325°F. Grease and flour a 9-inch ring mold, or an 8-inch cake pan.

2 Cream the butter and sugar until soft and light. Gradually beat in the eggs. Sift the flour and fold into the creamed mixture.

3 Drain the canned pineapple, setting aside 1 tablespoon of syrup for the frosting and 3 tablespoons of syrup for the cake. Chop the pineapple rings finely. Fold the dried fruit, nuts, and pineapple into the cake mixture with the coconut, golden raisins, and the 3 tablespoons of pineapple syrup.

4 Put the mixture into the ring mold or cake pan. Bake for 1¼ hours if using a ring mold and 1½ hours if using a cake pan. Allow the cake to cool for at least 10 minutes in the pan, then turn out on to a wire rack and leave to cool completely.

5 To make the frosting, melt the butter in a saucepan and then remove from the heat. Sift the confectioner's sugar into the butter, then add 1 tablespoon of pineapple syrup and the coconut. Stir to combine, then spread the frosting over the top of the cake and a little down the sides. Sprinkle with toasted coconut shavings.

3 **eggs**

⅓ cup **superfine sugar**, plus extra for sprinkling

½ cup **unbleached all-purpose flour**

scant ¼ cup **cocoa powder**

½ cup **heavy whipping cream**

⅔ cup **canned sweetened chestnut purée**

To decorate:

½ cup **heavy whipping cream**

7 oz **plain dark chocolate**, broken into pieces

3 **chocolate flakes**

confectioner's sugar, for dusting

Serves 10
*Preparation time: **40 minutes**,*
plus cooling
*Cooking time: **20 minutes***

Bûche de Noël

Chocolate flakes give this French Yule log an authentic-looking bark. The log can be made a day in advance or it can be frozen. Dust with sugar just before serving.

1 Preheat the oven to 350°F. Grease a 13 x 19-inch jelly roll pan and line it with parchment paper. Whisk the eggs and sugar in a heatproof bowl over a pan of hot water until the mixture leaves a trail when the beaters are lifted. Sift in the flour and cocoa powder and fold in with a metal spoon.

2 Pour the mixture into the prepared pan and spread it into the corners. Bake for about 15 minutes until just firm. Sprinkle a sheet of parchment paper with superfine sugar and invert the cake on to it. Peel away the baking paper that lined the pan, then roll up the sponge in the fresh paper and leave to cool.

3 To make the filling, whip the cream until softly peaking, then fold in the chestnut purée. Unroll the sponge and spread the

chestnut cream over the top. (Don't worry if the cake cracks, because the cracks won't show once the log is assembled.) Roll the cake back into a log shape.

4 To make the decoration, bring the cream almost to a boil in a small saucepan. Remove from the heat and stir in the chocolate pieces. Leave until melted, then stir until smooth. Allow to cool.

5 Arrange the cake, seam side down, on a serving plate. Lightly whip the chocolate cream to thicken it slightly, then spread it over the top and sides of the cake. Cut the flakes lengthwise into long pieces. Press them lightly on to the chocolate cream, filling in the gaps with smaller pieces of flake. To serve, dust the log liberally with confectioner's sugar.

Cherub cake

This elegant layered cake is sandwiched with creamy butter and jam and flavored with lime.

1 Preheat the oven to 325°F. Line the base and sides of an 8-inch, deep, round cake pan with parchment paper. Cream the margarine and sugar until light and fluffy. Beat in the eggs and flour alternately until smooth.

2 Stir in the lime zest and the juice from half a lime. Spoon into the prepared pan and level. Bake for 1–1¼ hours until well risen. Cool in the pan then turn out; peel off the paper and slice into three layers.

3 Beat the butter, confectioner's sugar and the remaining lime juice until smooth.

4 Sandwich cakes with butter cream and jam. Spread the remaining butter cream over top and sides.

5 Drape the rolled fondant over the cake. Gently press over the top and sides until smooth, using your fingertips dusted with a little confectioner's sugar. Trim excess.

6 Shape a small piece of modeling icing into a ball and press into a 2½ inch nonstick cherub icing mold. Invert mold and gently ease the shaped cherub out. Trim off excess icing. Transfer to a baking sheet lined with parchment. Continue until 8 cherubs have been made.

7 Roll out the remaining icing, then cut thin strips. Twist each one into a corkscrew, propping up the twists with pieces of crumpled foil. Leave overnight to dry.

8 Paint gold detail on cherub wings. Arrange on top of the cake, with the icing ribbons. Secure with a little water or white frosting from a tube. Add fabric ribbon to side.

¾ cup (1½ sticks) **margarine**

¾ cup **superfine sugar**

3 **eggs**

2¼ cups **self-rising flour**

finely grated zest of 2 **limes**

juice of 1½ **limes**

7 tablespoons **butter**, at room temperature

2 cups **confectioner's sugar**, plus extra for dusting

¼ cup **raspberry jam**

14½ oz ready-to-use **white rolled fondant**

8-oz tub **modeling icing paste**

edible **gold food coloring**

Serves 8
*Preparation time: **1½ hours***
*Cooking time: **1–1¼ hours***

½ cup **fresh cranberries**

2 tablespoons **superfine sugar**

1 large **pear**, peeled and sliced

whole berry **cranberry sauce**,
to serve

Cake:

¾ cup (1½ sticks) **butter**, at
room temperature

¾ cup **superfine sugar**

3 **eggs**

1¾ cups **self-rising flour**

finely grated zest of 1 **orange**

2 tablespoons **orange juice**

Serves 6–8
*Preparation time: **30 minutes***
*Cooking time: **1–1¼ hours***

Cranberry and pear upside-down cake

This is an ideal cake to make over the Christmas holidays, because it can be served warm with custard as a dessert, then cold the next day with mugs of coffee or tea.

1 Preheat the oven to 350°F. Grease an 8-inch, round springform pan and line with a circle of parchment paper. Sprinkle the cranberries and sugar over the base then arrange the pear slices on top.

2 To make the cake, cream the butter and sugar in a bowl until light and fluffy. Gradually beat in the eggs and flour until smooth, then mix in the orange zest and juice.

3 Spoon the cake mixture over the top of the pears, level the surface and cook for 1–1¼ hours until well risen and golden and a toothpick inserted into the center comes out clean. Check after 45 minutes and cover with foil if the cake appears to be browning too quickly.

4 Loosen the edges of the cake, cover it with a large plate, then invert the pan on to the plate and remove. Spoon a little cranberry sauce over the top while still hot. Serve warm or cold, cut into wedges with whipped cream and a dusting of sifted icing sugar.

TIP
Frozen cranberries can be used instead of fresh, but be sure to defrost them thoroughly first.

cakes 44

Toffee apple muffin

This makes a great standby and you will find that few people can resist it. During cooking, the sugar melts to form a deliciously smooth, toffee-like sauce for the apples. It is perfect served with homemade vanilla ice cream.

1 Preheat the oven to 425°F. Toss the apples in a shallow, ovenproof dish with 1 tablespoonful of the flour and the raw sugar.

2 Mix the remaining flour with the superfine sugar and mixed spice in a bowl. Add the egg, yogurt, and butter and stir lightly until only just combined.

3 Spoon the mixture over the apples and bake for 15–20 minutes until they are just firm and golden. Serve warm.

*To prepare mixed spice, combine ¼ teaspoon cinnamon, 2 teaspoons nutmeg, 1 teaspoon allspice, and 1 teaspoon ginger (optional). Store in a spice jar and use for apple pies and fruit crisps.

3 **dessert apples**, cored and thickly sliced

scant 1 cup **self-rising flour**, plus 1 tablespoon extra

½ cup **raw sugar**

¼ cup **superfine sugar**

½ teaspoon **ground mixed spice***

1 **egg**

½ cup **natural yogurt**

¼ cup (½ stick) unsalted **butter**, melted

Serves 4
*Preparation time: **10 minutes***
*Cooking time: **15–20 minutes***

3 teaspoons **cocoa powder**

3 teaspoons **boiling water**

½ cup (1 stick) soft **margarine** or **butter**, at room temperature

½ cup **superfine sugar**

1 cup plus 2 tablespoons **unbleached all-purpose flour**

To decorate:

1 oz **plain dark chocolate**, broken into pieces

⅓ cup (3⅓ oz) **dark chocolate**

3 teaspoons **cocoa powder**

3 teaspoons **boiling water**

¼ cup (½ stick) **butter**, at room temperature

scant 1 cup **confectioner's sugar**

6 **candied cherries**

1 small package of **candy-coated chocolates**

Makes 12
*Preparation time: **40 minutes***
*Cooking time: **13–15 minutes***

Reindeer cupcakes

These fun-sized chocolate cupcakes will bring a festive smile to the face of any small child. They are decorated with chocolates and candied cherries for an authentic Rudolph nose.

1 Preheat the oven to 350°F. Line a 12-cup muffin pan with paper baking cups. Put the cocoa powder into a bowl and mix to a smooth paste with the boiling water.

2 Put all the remaining cake ingredients into a bowl and beat until smooth. Stir in the cocoa paste then divide the mixture between the baking cups. Bake the cupcakes for 13–15 minutes until they are well risen and spring back when pressed with a fingertip. Leave to cool.

3 Meanwhile, place the chocolate in a heatproof bowl and melt over a saucepan of gently simmering water. Spoon melted chocolate into a greaseproof paper piping bag, snip off the tip, and pipe lines of chocolate around 2½ inches long on a baking tray lined with nonstick baking paper. Pipe on small branches for antlers. Make enough for two per cake with extras in case of breakages. Leave to dry and harden.

4 Mix the cocoa powder with the boiling water in a large bowl. Add the butter then gradually beat in the confectioner's sugar to make a smooth frosting. Spread the frosting over the tops of the cupcakes. Add a halved cherry for a nose and 2 little candies for eyes, piping on the remaining melted chocolate to make eyeballs. Peel the antlers off the parchment paper and stick at angles into the cupcakes. Store the cupcakes in a cool place until ready to serve.

½ cup (1 stick) **butter**

½ cup **maple syrup**

½ cup **raw sugar**

2 cups **self-rising flour**

1 teaspoon **baking powder**

1 teaspoon **ground ginger**

2 **eggs**

½ cup **milk**

3 tablespoons **candied ginger**, chopped, plus extra to decorate

Frosting:

1¾ cups **confectioner's sugar**, sifted

4 teaspoons **water**

2 pieces **candied ginger**, sliced

Makes 12
*Preparation time: **30 minutes**, plus setting*
*Cooking time: **10–15 minutes***

Snow-covered ginger muffins

Light, moist and very tasty, these frosting-crowned muffins taste delicious with a mug of steaming cappuccino or hot chocolate.

1 Preheat the oven to 350°F. Line 12 cups of a deep muffin pan with paper baking cups. Put the butter, syrup, and sugar into a saucepan and heat gently, stirring until the butter has melted. Mix the flour, baking powder, and ground ginger in a bowl. Beat the eggs and milk in another bowl.

2 Take the butter pan off the heat, then beat in the flour mixture. Gradually beat in the egg and milk mixture, then stir in the candied ginger. Divide the mixture evenly into the baking cups and bake for 10–15 minutes until well risen and cracked. Leave to cool.

3 Sift the icing sugar into a bowl and gradually mix in the water to create a smooth spoonable frosting. Drizzle random lines of frosting from a spoon over the muffins and complete with slices of ginger. Leave to harden for 30 minutes before serving.

7 oz **white chocolate**, broken into pieces

½ cup (1 stick) **butter**

3 **eggs**

¾ cup **superfine sugar**

1 teaspoon **vanilla extract**

1⅓ cups **unbleached all-purpose flour**

1 teaspoon **baking powder**

⅓ cup **dried cranberries**

Makes 20
Preparation time: **25 minutes**
Cooking time: **20–25 minutes**

Cranberry blondies

These moist white-chocolate brownies, packed with chunky pieces of white chocolate and ruby-red cranberries, are a terrific seasonal treat.

1 Preheat the oven to 350°F. Line a 7 x 11 x 2-inch roasting pan with a large piece of parchment paper and snip diagonally into the corners so that the paper fits snugly over the base and up the sides of the pan.

2 Place half of the chocolate and the butter in a heatproof bowl and melt over a saucepan of gently simmering water. Whisk the eggs, sugar, and vanilla in a separate bowl with an electric whisk until light and frothy and the whisk leaves a trail when lifted above the mixture.

3 Fold the melted chocolate and butter mixture into the beaten eggs with a large metal spoon. Sift the flour and baking powder over the top and then fold in gently. Chop the remaining chocolate and fold half of it into the mixture with half the cranberries.

4 Pour the mixture into the lined pan and sprinkle with the rest of the diced chocolate and cranberries. Bake for 30–35 minutes until well risen; the top of the cake should be crusty and golden and the center still slightly soft. Leave to cool in the pan. Lift the paper and cake out of the pan, peel off the paper and cut into squares to serve.

TIP
Many roasting pans have sloping sides, so measure the base dimensions when choosing one.

½ cup (1 stick) **butter**

½ cup **raw sugar**

½ cup **heavy whipping cream**

3 **eggs**

⅓ cup **superfine sugar**

1⅓ cups **unbleached all-purpose flour**

1 teaspoon **baking powder**

Frosting:

¼ cup (½ stick) **butter**

scant ⅓ cup **raw sugar**

¼ cup **heavy whipping cream**

3 oz **plain dark chocolate**, broken into pieces

Makes 15
Preparation time: **25 minutes**, *plus cooling*
Cooking time: **25–30 minutes**

Butterscotch brownies

Everyone will be clamoring for seconds with these wonderfully light, toffee brownies.

1 Preheat the oven to 350°F. Line a 7 x 11 x 2-inch roasting pan with a large piece of parchment paper and snip diagonally into the corners so that the paper fits snugly over the base and up the sides of the pan.

2 Put the butter and sugar into a small saucepan and heat gently until the butter has melted and the sugar has dissolved. Take off the heat and stir in the cream. Whisk the eggs and superfine sugar in a bowl until light and frothy and the whisk leaves a trail when lifted out of the mixture.

3 Fold the butterscotch mixture into the beaten eggs using a large metal spoon. Sift the flour and baking powder over the top then fold in gently. Pour into the lined pan. Bake for 25–30 minutes until well risen; the top should be crusty and the center just set. Leave to cool for 15 minutes.

4 Lift the brownies out of the pan by holding the paper lining, place on a wire rack and peel the paper away from the sides. To make the frosting, heat the butter and sugar in a saucepan until the sugar has dissolved and the butter has melted. Add the cream and stir over medium heat for 2 minutes. Pour over the brownies and spread into an even layer—don't worry if a little drizzles down the sides. Leave to cool for 15 minutes.

5 Place the chocolate in a heatproof bowl and melt over a saucepan of gently simmering water. Drizzle random squiggles over the butterscotch frosting then leave the brownies to cool completely. Cut into squares and peel off the parchment paper.

Cranberry, oatmeal, and cinnamon scones

These sweet, cranberry-speckled scones are best served freshly baked. Alternatively, make them in advance, freeze, and warm through before serving.

1 Preheat the oven to 425°F and grease a baking sheet. Place the flour, baking powder, and cinnamon in a food processor. Add the butter and process until the mixture resembles breadcrumbs. Add the sugar and oatmeal and blend briefly. Alternatively, use your fingertips to rub the butter into the flour, baking powder, and cinnamon in a bowl, then add the sugar and oatmeal.

2 Add the cranberries and milk and blend briefly until the mixture forms a soft dough, adding a little more milk if necessary. Turn out on to a floured surface and roll out to a ¾-inch thickness. Cut out rounds using a 2-inch cutter. Transfer to the prepared baking sheet and reroll the trimmings to make more scones.

3 Brush the scones with beaten egg or milk and sprinkle with oatmeal. Bake for 10–12 minutes until risen and golden, then transfer to a wire rack to cool. Serve split and buttered.

1½ cups **self-rising flour**

1 teaspoon **baking powder**

1 teaspoon **ground cinnamon**

6 tablespoons unsalted **butter**, cut into small pieces

⅓ cup **superfine sugar**

¼ cup **oatmeal**, plus extra for sprinkling

⅓ cup **dried cranberries**

5–6 tablespoons **milk**

beaten **egg** or **milk**, to glaze

Makes 10
*Preparation time: **10 minutes***
*Cooking time: **10–12 minutes***

8 oz **puff pastry**, thawed if frozen

flour, for dusting

1 **egg yolk**

2 tablespoons **milk**

18 squares of **plain dark chocolate**

1 teaspoon grated **orange zest**

1 pinch of **ground star anise**

butter, for greasing

Makes 9
Preparation time: **15 minutes**
Cooking time: **12 minutes**

Spiced chocolate pastries

Oozing with molten chocolate, these are delicious with a mug of tea or freshly brewed coffee.

1 Preheat the oven to 400°F and grease a baking sheet. Roll out the pastry thinly on a lightly floured surface and trim to form a 9-inch square. Cut into thirds crossways and lengthwise to form 9 squares.

2 Beat the egg yolk and milk to make a glaze and brush a little around the edges of each pastry square. Place 2 squares of chocolate, a little orange zest, and a touch of star anise on each one. Fold diagonally in half and press the edges together to seal.

3 Place the pastries on the prepared baking sheet and cook for 12 minutes, until risen and golden. Leave them to cool on a wire rack for a few minutes before serving.

Layered nutty bars

These no-bake chocolate refrigerator bars can be mixed quickly and then left to chill. Serve as part of an afternoon tea or cut into tiny bite-sized pieces to make petits fours.

¼ cup (½ stick) **butter**

1 13-oz can **fat free sweetened condensed milk**

7 oz **plain dark chocolate**, broken into pieces

½ cup (4 oz) **shortbread cookies**

¼ cup **hazelnuts**

heaping ⅓ cup **pistachio nuts**

Serves 10
Preparation time: **20 minutes**, plus chilling
Cooking time: **3–4 minutes**

1 Use a little of the butter to grease the base and sides of an 8-inch round springform pan. Put the rest of the butter into a saucepan with the condensed milk and chocolate. Heat gently for 3–4 minutes, stirring until melted, then remove from heat.

2 Put the shortbread into a plastic bag and roughly crush into chunky pieces with a rolling pin. Toast the hazelnuts under a preheated hot grill until lightly browned, then roughly chop with the pistachios.

3 Stir the shortbread into the chocolate mixture then spoon half the mixture into the prepared pan and spread flat. Reserve 2 tablespoons of the nuts for the top, then sprinkle the rest over the chocolate biscuit layer. Cover with the remaining chocolate mixture, level the top with the back of the spoon and sprinkle with the reserved nuts.

4 Chill the nut mixture for 3–4 hours until firm, then loosen the edge of the pan and remove the sides. Cut into thin slices. Any leftovers can be stored in the refrigerator, wrapped in foil, for up to 3 days.

TIP
Candied cherries or ginger, golden raisins or dried apricots can also be added instead of some of the nuts.

¼ cup **blanched hazelnuts**

½ cup (1 stick) **butter**, softened, plus extra for greasing

¼ cup **superfine sugar**

1⅓ cups **unbleached all-purpose flour**

Makes 20
Preparation time: **10 minutes**
Cooking time: **12 minutes**

Quick hazelnut melts

These hazelnut cookies literally melt in your mouth.

1 Preheat the oven to 375°F and grease a baking sheet. Grind the hazelnuts in a food processor or blender until fairly smooth but still retaining a little texture. Brown in a heavy-based frying pan over low heat until evenly golden. Pour into a bowl and stir until cool.

2 Blend the butter and sugar in a food processor until creamy. Add the flour and cooled nuts and blend again to make a soft dough.

3 Take walnut-sized pieces of dough and shape into balls, then pat into flat ovals. Place on the greased baking sheet and flatten slightly with a fork. Bake for 12 minutes, until just golden. Cool on a wire rack. These little cakes can be stored in an airtight container for up to 3 days.

2 teaspoons **cocoa powder**, plus extra to garnish

2 tablespoons (1 fl oz) **Kahlua coffee liqueur**

⅓ cup **hot brewed coffee**

mini marshmallows

whipped cream

Serves 1
*Preparation time: **5 minutes***
*Cooking time: **3 minutes***

Marshmallow mocha

An indulgent, chocolatey version of Irish coffee, with melted marshmallows and whipped cream on top. This makes a great follow-up to a light dessert at a dinner party.

1 Put the cocoa powder in a toddy glass, add the Kahlua and coffee and stir until mixed. Drop in the mini marshmallows and float the cream on top. Garnish with a sprinkling of cocoa powder.

Festive hot chocolate

Thick and luscious hot chocolate topped with a frothy white cloud of cream and melting marshmallows is wonderfully indulgent and heart-warming. If you really want to spoil yourself, add a few tablespoons of brandy.

1 Pour the milk into a saucepan and bring just to a boil. Remove the pan from heat and add the chocolate, sugar, cinnamon, and marshmallows. Let stand for 2–3 minutes.

2 Meanwhile, whip the cream in a bowl until it is just beginning to thicken and form soft peaks. Using a whisk, beat the milk mixture in the saucepan until frothy. Pour into cups or mugs and spoon the cream on top.

3 Decorate each cup or mug with a few extra marshmallows and a sprinkling of cinnamon. Serve immediately.

2½ cups **whole milk**

3½ oz **plain dark chocolate**, broken into pieces

¼ cup **superfine sugar**

a little **ground cinnamon**

½ cup **marshmallows**, plus extra to serve

½ cup **heavy whipping cream**

Makes 4 cups or 2 large mugs
*Preparation time: **5 minutes***
*Cooking time: **3 minutes***

crushed **ice**

6 cups **cranberry juice**

2 cups **orange juice**

2 cups **ginger ale**

cocktail cherries, lemon slices, and **lime spirals**, to decorate

Serves 15
*Preparation time: **5 minutes***

Cranberry crush

A tempting fruit punch with a seasonal theme, perfect for Christmas parties with all age groups.

1 Half-fill a punch bowl with crushed ice. Pour in the cranberry and orange juices and stir to mix. Fill to the brim with the ginger ale and decorate with cocktail cherries, lemon slices, and lime spirals. Serve immediately.

TIP
For a special party, float red rose petals on the top of the punch.

---

6 tablespoons **grenadine**

6 tablespoons **vodka**

seeds from 1 **pomegranate**

1 **lime**, thinly sliced (optional)

1 bottle **sparkling dry white wine**, well chilled

Serves 6
*Preparation time: **5 minutes***

Pomegranate punch

This vibrant pink punch looks innocent enough but has a hidden kick, so warn drivers and children to steer clear.

1 Divide the grenadine and vodka between 6 champagne flutes, then add the pomegranate seeds and lime slices (if using). Top up with the sparkling wine and serve at once.

TIPS
To remove the pomegranate seeds, cut the pomegranate in half, then break it into pieces and pop out the pink seeds. For a less alcoholic punch, half-fill the glasses with cranberry and apple juice, then add the vodka and a little less wine.

3½ cups **orange juice**

7 cups **purple grape juice**

juice of 6 **lemons**

juice of 6 **limes**

sugar syrup, to taste

20–30 **ice cubes**

orange, **lemon** and **lime** slices, to decorate

Serves 15
Preparation time: 5 minutes

2 tablespoons **brandy**

2 tablespoons **dark rum**

1 **egg**

1 teaspoon **sugar syrup**

⅓ cup **whole milk**

grated **nutmeg**, to decorate

Serves 1
Preparation time: 5 minutes

Holiday sangria

Sangria puts everyone into a holiday mood. This non-alcoholic version is thirst-quenching and delicious.

1 Pour the orange juice into a punch bowl. Add the grape, lemon, and lime juices and stir to mix. Add sugar syrup to taste and stir well. Add the ice, then float the fruit slices on top.

TIP
To make sugar syrup, boil equal quantities of sugar and water until the sugar has dissolved then allow to cool.

FOR ALCOHOLIC SANGRIA
Substitute red wine for the grape juice and add ¾ cup of brandy.

Egg nog

This traditional winter drink served dusted with grated nutmeg will bring out the Christmas spirit in anyone. Serve to special guests.

1 Put the brandy, rum, egg, and sugar syrup into a cocktail shaker and shake well, then strain into a large goblet. Add the milk, stir gently, then decorate with a little grated nutmeg.

Index

Executive Editor: Sarah Ford
Project Editor: Kate Tuckett
Executive Art Editor: Joanna MacGregor
Designer: Darren Southern
Production Controller: Nigel Reed
Food stylist: Sara Lewis
Special Photography: Lis Parsons/
© Octopus Publishing Group Ltd